D1490060

The Way of the Journal:
A Journal Therapy
Workbook for Healing

Kathleen Adams, MA, LPC

The Sidran Institute Press

200 East Joppa Road, Suite 207

Baltimore, Maryland 21286

410.825.8888 www.sidran.org

This book is designed to provide information in regard to the subject matter covered. It is sold with the understanding that the publisher and author are not engaged in providing psychological or professional services through this medium. If such professional advice or service is required, the services of a competent professional should be sought. The purpose of this workbook is to educate, inform, and enlighten those persons who wish to use a personal process journal for self-understanding, or those who may be working with such individuals professionally. The author and Sidran Institute Press will have neither liability nor responsibility to any person or entity with respect to any loss or damage caused, or alleged to be caused, directly or indirectly, by the information in this book.

ISBN 978-0-9629164-2-7
Printed in the United States of America

Dedicated to all of the students, clients, and friends
who have participated in my work since 1985
and especially to the writing group known as
Scribe 1990–1992

Acknowledgments

Thanks to the team who supported the **Scribe** program at The National Center for the Treatment of Dissociative Disorders: Walter C. Young, MD; Becky Rudolph, MS; Nancy Cole, PsyD; Mary Ann Bolkovatz, RN, MS, CS; Trish Knode, ATR, LPC; Sarah Becker, ADTR, LPC; Del Crothers, RN; Anne Clark, MA; Doug Maxey; Michael Crothers; and all the clinicians and staff. Thanks to Bruce Brooks, MDiv for his superb co-facilitation of **Scribe** and to Carol Hanson for introducing Walter to journal therapy and me to Walter. Special thanks to Walter C. Young, MD for his mentorship, vision and support of my work. Most of all, thanks to the patients who participated in **Scribe** and thus helped write this book.

Table of Contents

Foreword

Beset as we are by myriad new ideas, technologies, therapies, health advice, and herbal remedies, it may be difficult to notice that many of the more enduring health practices are based on profoundly simple human acts. Zen meditation, for example, brings our attention to nothing more complicated or unusual than our breathing, yoga to the stretching of our body, Tai Chi to our movement through space. Each gives rise to a mindfulness about our presence as human beings. Yet each requires some discipline and guidance, and regular practice, despite how simple breathing, stretching, and moving appear to be.

Kay Adams, in this wonderful revision of *The Way of the Journal,* brings our attention to another basic human act: writing. Like meditation or quiet reflection, journaling appreciates the value of processing our feelings and thoughts, allowing them to flow out of us, and revealing the widsom, memory, and suffering they contain. Like all deeply human acts, writing is steeped in paradox: we write simultaneously for ourselves and for others; we write as authors so that we can read as audience; we write to empty our minds of troubling thoughts and also to record them for posterity.

Kay Adams is the perfect person to offer such a book as *The Way of the Journal,* because she loves to write, and yet respects these paradoxes of writing. Throughout this book, one feels her commitment to care for, guide, and accompany the reader on a journey that she herself has fully embraced. She speaks with great clarity, inspiration, and balance. For she has discoverd some pitfalls, darkened corners, and detours in this journey that have made some travelers turn back.

"What? I need no help to *write* (an inner voice calls)! Let me plunge, like the hero, alone, free, into the well of my unconscious! Let me wrestle with the tiger, the demons, that guard my treasured spirit!" No, Kay warns, such unbridled enthusiasm may lead paradoxically to a reduction of freedom, an impasse constructed by one's internal critical voice. One *does* need a guide to successfully enter the inner world. *The Way of the Journal* is just such a guide. Kay's developmental approach to journaling offers thoughtfully constructed exercises that are helpful with *specific* moods and issues. The book abounds with unique insights. Her work reflects some of the most sophisticated thinking about journaling in the field today.

It is often said that the experienced sailor is not the one who can handle his ship in any weather, against any current or tide, but rather is the one whose ship is rarely caught by surprise, who knows when to take down the sails or even stay in port. For the experienced sailor *knows* the sea, its winds and tides and currents. Like the experienced sailor, Kay Adams has a deep respect for the power of her particular sea, and so one can trust that the journey will go well.

As a result, Kay has succeeded in producing an exceptionally useful journal therapy workbook for clients, therapists, and teachers. This revised edition has many improvements that offer clear, thoughtful, and flexibile ideas for journaling, embedded within a

sophisticated approach to healing. Creativity, sensitivity, and delight spring forth from every page! I highly recommend this workbook to all who have found themselves jotting down their thoughts, whether in diaries, on the back of envelopes, or cash register receipts! *The Way of the Journal* will help transform these nascent efforts into the rich, therapeutic exploration that process writing can be.

David Read Johnson, Ph.D.
Director, The Institutes for the Arts in Psychotherapy, New York, NY
Co-Cirector, Post Traumatic Stress Center, New Haven, CT

To All Who Write Or Want To

In 1985 I had the good sense to answer the door when my destiny came knocking, and since then my passion — some might say my obsession —has been journals and their people. I teach, write, consult, facilitate, research, lecture, publish and give trainings on journal therapy, the use of reflective or process writing as a tool for psychological growth and emotional healing.

As you might imagine, I've read a lot of journals and heard a lot of stories. And while no two journals are ever alike, over the years the stories have grown familiar. Like modern myths acted out on the nakedness of pages, these stories have taken on an almost archetypal depth.

There are the invasion-of-privacy stories: *My mother (or teacher, son, partner, therapist, minister, neighbor, lawyer, etc.) read my journal and used it to humiliate (or threaten, make fun of, belittle, ridicule, intimidate, etc.) me. My boundaries were violated; my personal space was invaded.*

There are the paper-trail stories: *If I'm not supposed to **talk** about my family secrets, why on earth would I **write them down?** Don't you know what might happen if this stuff fell into the wrong hands? Do you take me for a fool?*

There are the wistful-poet stories: *I've always wanted to write but I'm no good, I flunked English, I'm not creative, nothing ever comes out right, there are too many people living in my head, I don't know how, I can't spell, I'm too afraid, I don't have time, but . . . **I've always wanted to write!***

The stories echo on and on, becoming richer and more resonant with the telling, until they finally come together in collective voice:

I was violated.

I was punished.

I was shamed.

Not all the stories are painful. There are true-companion stories: *Where would I be without my journal, I can't overestimate its value, it's the only place I can be me, nobody better touch it, it's my lifeline, it's my sacred space.*

And stories of the Mysteries: *I sometimes sense something good, I tell myself Truth, an angel just sat on my shoulder, I don't know how I know, it just seems to write itself, I somehow feel more whole.*

These voices, too, swell in chorus:

I am loved.

I am not alone.

Whether you sing alto or soprano, a journal is sheet music to the choir. May our voices rise as one.

Kathleen Adams, MA, LPC
Clinical Journal Therapist
Denver, Colorado May 1993

In the four years since *The Way of the Journal* was published, there has been a controlled explosion in the field of journal therapy.

Membership in The National Association for Poetry Therapy, the professional organization for those who work with the interface among writing, literature, poetics and healing, has nearly doubled. More than half of the books in this edition's suggested reading list, representing "the best of the best" of the literature about therapeutic writing, have been published in this decade, with 27% published since 1993. The internet has birthed a whole new genre of on-line journalkeeping, with diarists of many cultures offering global windows of paradoxically anonymous intimacy.

Throughout it all, The Center for Journal Therapy has held a steady vision of making the healing art of journal writing accessible to all who desire self-directed change. Hundreds of psychotherapists have now attended the Clinical Journal Therapy trainings. Our professional programs have expanded to include Journal the Healing Journey, a training for holistic health practitioners and medical personnel. My own work has taken me more deeply into the stories of our lives as they create themselves through personal mythology, spiritual autobiography, life-based fiction and narrative therapy.

The Way of the Journal, originally written as the outcome of my work with sexual trauma survivors, has proved itself to be a theoretical and developmental model useful for people in recovery from all types of traumatic stress, as well as those who have had a difficult time getting started with a therapeutic writing program, and for therapists who wish to offer a clinically sound approach to writing. Letters from readers and users all over the country confirm that the workbook is doing what it set out to do: Offer a practical, pragmatic, theoretically grounded way to use journal therapy techniques and interventions for the healing of body, psyche and soul.

This second edition offers new theoretical ideas on the journal ladder, a developmental approach to journal therapy, and thumbnail sketches of the journal interventions that are not specifically practiced within the workbook. There is a new section on working with dreams in the journal, and many of the workbook pages have been updated to enhance the user's success with the techniques.

The vital tools of structure, pacing and containment continue to dominate the theoretical ground of this workbook, and I am more convinced than ever of their necessity in a holistic approach to therapeutic writing. A popular writing practice these days is "morning pages," a daily three-page free-write to be done immediately upon awakening. Again and again I have heard stories from clients and clinicians about depressives and traumatic stress survivors whose struggles intensified with morning pages. When this phenomenon is viewed through the lens of the developmental continuum and the tools of structure, pacing and containment, it quickly makes sense. Extended stream-of-consciousness writing first thing in the morning, when the membrane between the conscious and unconscious minds is most permeable, is a high-level journal therapy intervention that may not serve those whose "first

voice" is often critical or fear-based. Applying the guidelines of structure, pacing and containment quickly shifts the focus and alleviates potential problems. When clients follow suggestions to write one page instead of three, or walk the dog first (or shower or eat breakfast), or write "evening pages," or intentionally bring in the balance of positive or humorous news, they report remarkable shifts back to writing that guides and resolves.

I am grateful for the calm, clear commitment of Esther Giller and The Sidran Foundation as this work continues its journey into the world. And above all I give thanks to Spirit, to which I surrender word by word and from which all pages flow.

Kathleen Adams, MA, LPC
Director, The Center for Journal Therapy
Denver, Colorado
www.journaltherapy.com
November 5, 1997

The Journal Ladder

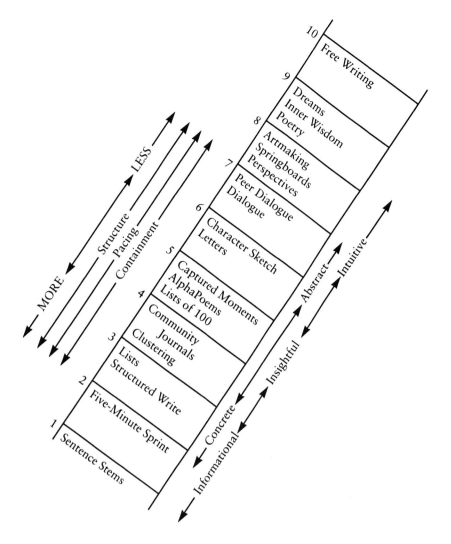

Structure:	Foundation, form, sequenced tasks, orderliness
Pacing:	Rhythm, movement, timing
Containment:	Boundaries, limits
Concrete:	Easy to grasp or implement, realistic
Abstract:	Symbolic, metaphoric, multidimensional
Informational:	Practical, immediately useful
Insightful:	Connections, patterns, awarenesses
Intuitive:	"Aha" experience, sudden knowing, internal wisdom

The journal ladder (see pp. 1–2) is a visual interpretation of the developmental continuum theory. It ranks the most frequently used journal therapy interventions onto progressive "rungs" that start with maximum structure, pacing and containment, and gradually move toward insight, fluidity and openness. Balance and permission are built into each stage. The continuum ends with free writing, where most people begin.

The lower numbers represent ways to write that are well structured, concrete, practical and immediately useful. As you move up the ladder, the techniques become increasingly more abstract, insightful, and intuitive The lower range is good when you're feeling overwhelmed, want information quickly, or don't have much time. The midrange is good for uncovering patterns and connections. The upper range is good for connecting with inner guidance and creativity.

From *The Way of the Journal*, © Kathleen Adams (1998, Sidran Press)   xi

Not all the techniques on the journal ladder are represented in this workbook. Following are brief descriptions of the other techniques, which are described in my book JOURNAL TO THE SELF.

Sentence Stems: See Day One

Five-Minute Sprint: See Day Two

Structured Write: See Day Three

Lists: Start thinking of your "to-do" lists as journal entries. Lists are pragmatic and efficient, and they can't be beat for gathering quick information.

Clustering: See Day Four

Community Journal: Consider keeping an ongoing communication book with your spouse, roommate, lover or kids. Keep it in a neutral and accessible location. Use it as an ongoing forum for expression of opinion, emotion, point of view or negotiation.

List of 100: A surefire way to clarify thoughts, identify patterns, dive below the surface, get past the obvious and quickly gather data. Repetition is an important part of the process; allow yourself to write the next thing in your mind, even if it's already on the list several times. Write words and phrases to make the list go faster. Just get it down as quickly as possible. When you're done, go back and find the themes.

AlphaPoems: See Day Five

Captured Moments: Vignettes capturing the sensations of a particularly meaningful or emotional experience. Captured Moments are sensual; pull out all the stops and stretch for the most descriptive adjectives and verbs you can find. A collection of Captured Moments becomes like a written photo album, preserving memories for the future.

Unsent Letters: Because letters are intentionally a one-way communication, they're a good choice when you have something to say and want to say it without interruption. Unsent Letters, often used effectively to discharge strong emotion, are a way of being safely out of control.

Character Sketch: See Day Six

Dialogue: See Day Seven

Peer Dialogue: A conflict-resolution dialogue in which you, in imagery, create a relationship of equals by adjusting the power dynamics between you and your dialogue partner. With a level playing field, free of the top dog/underdog dynamics of real life, you can create parity long enough to communicate as equals.

Perspectives: An alteration in point of view that provides a different perspective on an event or situation. Write in the third person about yourself, write as if you were someone else, or propel yourself backward or forward in time.

Springboards: See Day Eight

Artmaking: Giving form, shape and color to your thoughts and feelings is another way of communicating with yourself. Art offers a visual metaphor that helps you see the context of your thoughts and feelings. If you can't draw or paint, try collage. Or paste pictures or images in your journal and write about what they evoke in you.

Poetry: See Day Nine

Inner Wisdom Dialogue: See Day Seven.

Dreams: Your life becomes transparent when you start paying attention to what goes on in your unconscious moments. Writing down your dreams is the first step. From there, use any number of journal devices: Cluster your dream symbols, Dialogue with your dream characters, write your best guess about the dream in a Five-Minute Sprint.

Free Writing: See Day Ten

Jump-Starting The Journal: The Developmental Continuum Of Journal Therapy

What's wrong with this picture?

- In a recent study[1], 88% of post-traumatic stress disordered (PTSD) clients said they wrote in a journal regularly (60%) or intermittently (28%).

- 64% started their present journal process in the context of therapy, 12-step recovery, psychiatric hospitalization or other therapeutic intervention.

- 56% shared their journals with their therapists.

So far, so good. Clients were writing and sharing journals; therapists were recommending and receiving them. So what's wrong with this picture?

- **96% felt fearful, frustrated, overwhelmed, insecure, intimidated, traumatized, ashamed or bored with their journals!** Only 4% said they did not experience obstacles, blocks or barriers to satisfying journalkeeping.

In practically every case, to a greater or lesser degree, the journal process contributed to chaos, internal struggle, consumption of emotional energy, compulsivity, affective flooding, overstimulation or disempowerment. The discomfort was so high that many clients perceived the journal as a sort of psychoid cod liver oil: The cure was worse than what ailed 'em.

So what's wrong with this picture? I asked myself. Here we had a resource with virtually unlimited potential as a therapeutic tool, and it was behaving paradoxically. Instead of empowering, it reduced. Instead of resolving, it provoked. Instead of working through, it overwhelmed. What was happening? And what could be done about it?

The first thing I looked at was *how* these clients were writing. I found that in the absence of suggestion or idea to the contrary, most sat down with a blank page or computer screen and blasted away — or tried to.

Small wonder they were having difficulties. Free writing is unboundaried, unstructured, open-ended, non-directed. When it is appropriately used, free writing can be a highly effective technique that offers clarity, insight, and intuitive connection. But it's not the technique of choice for either end of the post-traumatic stress continuum. In the hyperarousal part of the PTSD cycle, free writing feels uncontrolled and oceanic; in the numbing part of the cycle, it feels flat and empty.

What's the opposite of free writing? I wondered. *If unstructured, uncontained, unpaced writing is at one end of a continuum, what's at the other end?*

---

[1] Adams K., "The Structured Journal Therapy Assessment: A Report on 50 Cases," *The Journal of Poetry Therapy*: Vol. 10, No. 2, Winter 1996.

Something . . . structured. Contained. Paced. Quick. Easy.

The developmental continuum of journal therapy — the Journals Quick and Easy method — is a ten-step ladder that starts with the most highly structured, highly contained, highly paced journal technique (Sentence Stems) and gradually builds in fluidity and openness. The continuum *ends* with free writing, where most people *begin*.

With the foundation of structure, pacing and containment in place, you can learn to match your mood, issue or desired outcome with a journal intervention that enhances the likelihood of success. You'll learn, for instance, that highly charged emotional states are served by techniques that maximize containment, such as Clustering or 5-Minute Sprints; that a sense of internal chaos or disorganization is soothed with the structure of AlphaPoems or Sentence Stems; and that overwhelming feelings can be managed with the pacing of the Structured Writing Exercise. You'll also learn that when you want to access inner wisdom or intuition, you can go up the scale to the more insight-oriented techniques — Character Sketch, Dialogue, Springboards, Poetry and, yes, Free Writing.

Out of ten techniques, you'll probably find there are two or three you especially like, two or three you don't particularly care for, and several in the middle. With a little practice, you'll learn to approach your most difficult or painful treatment issues with journal interventions that are most likely to predict success.

What if you're not dealing with PTSD? It still works. Since I discovered the developmental continuum approach, I've used it with several other clinical populations. It seems to be an effective, solid bridge into journalkeeping for just about every emotional difficulty.

The poet Richard Solly once observed that journalkeeping requires courage and sweaters. Courage because it's often hard and painful to see your life before you in black and white; sweaters because we all need something to cozy up to. My hope for you is that this workbook will offer real courage and metaphoric sweaters. May you be warm and safe and brave.

A Note To
Therapists

The Way of the Journal was the outcome of many requests from clients and therapists alike for immediately useful skills and practical education in the use of process writing as a therapeutic tool.

The Way of the Journal teaches ten different journal techniques helpful to people in treatment for a wide variety of emotional difficulties. The workbook teaches vital tools for creating a positive journal relationship, including balance, permission and choice-making.

The workbook can be completed in less than 30 minutes a day over about a two-week period. After each day's entry the "So, how was it?" section provides a place to evaluate the journal technique used. This helps both the client and the therapist identify those techniques that will be most helpful as ongoing therapeutic interventions. The small springboard questions at the bottom of the daily pages are designed to bring balance into the journal by drawing focus toward normalization, future orientation and even whimsy. *If the client is willing,* it's useful if the therapist and client can review the workbook together upon completion.

If you intend to use this material with your clients, please complete the workbook yourself. You will be able to more appropriately help your clients if you use this workbook as a laboratory for your own journal exploration. Ask Sidran Press for information on bulk rates if you want to keep an inventory of workbooks on hand for your clients.

Journal therapists are professionally associated through The National Association for Poetry Therapy (NAPT), Dept. CJT, PO Box 551, Port Washington, NY, 11050. If you are using journals in your work with clients, I encourage you to consider membership in this interdisciplinary organization. Credentialing in both developmental and clinical poetry/journal therapy is offered through NAPT.

I am very interested in your feedback, suggestions, experiences and questions about this workbook. Please write me at The Center for Journal Therapy, PO Box 963, Arvada, CO 80001.

How To Use This Workbook

The Way of the Journal is designed to give you, the journal-keeper, some basic journal skills in as little as two weeks, with a commitment of up to 30 minutes a day spent in focused journal work. You'll gain maximum benefit if you start with Day One and proceed straight on through to Day Ten, without skipping anything, rearranging the order, or bailing out in the middle.

Above all else, please very gently remove all of your "I can't write" tapes and stack them carefully away. If you still want them when you're finished, they'll be here waiting.

Now for some specific ideas about using the workbook:

1. *The Way of the Journal* is designed to go from *short, structured, contained* journal entries to *loose, open-ended, unstructured* journal entries. The workbook's design minimizes the risk of overstimulation or flooding and offers several different approaches to the journal that can be used for a wide variety of issues and applications.

2. Commit to doing the workbook as a process. Plan to complete it once you begin.

3. Read Section I, *The 79¢ Therapist,* from my book JOURNAL TO THE SELF for ideas and information about permission, "rules," etc. More detailed information on some of the writing techniques is contained in JOURNAL's Section II, *The Journal Toolbox.*

4. Do the writing tasks directly on the blank workbook page following each exercise. When you've finished the writing, come back to the daily page and complete the "So, how was it?" section. Use this space to reflect on the writing technique and process you've just finished. Was the technique effective for you? Did your writing surprise you? What new insights or awarenesses did you gain? Would you use this technique again?

5. Also do the daily Springboard at the bottom of the page. These little wanderings are designed to show you that your writing doesn't always have to be intense, heavy or process-oriented. Daily musings are the twine that bind a journal to itself.

6. **Don't push yourself beyond the place you can realistically go.** This workbook is designed to teach you how to work safely and effectively in a journal. Pace yourself by choosing subjects to write about that will give you a good stretch without pulling any muscles. Writing is like running. The warm-up and the cool-down are as important as the run.

7. Some other DON'Ts: Don't expect yourself to be perfect. Don't share your journal with anyone you don't want to, including your therapist, and you don't have to explain why. There's no "right" way to do it, so don't assume you're doing it "wrong." Don't feel bound by "rules" (such as "I should write every day" or "I should

do the steps in order") unless you happen to like them or otherwise find them useful.

8. Some DOs: Do give yourself a chance. Do trust that you have a voice, that it can be heard, and that it falls on compassionate ears. If you have a chance, do join a journal group or class and experience the special qualities of writing in community. Do hug your journal.

The Way of the Journal is self-paced from here. I want to hear your journal stories, your successes, your questions, your experiences with the workbook and beyond. You can write me directly at The Center for Journal Therapy, PO Box 963, Arvada, CO 80001.

Getting Ready To Write

When you are getting ready to do any sort of process work in your journal, it is important to **empower yourself** by creating an environment that feels safe, comfortable and nurturing. The following list, created by journal group participants, gives suggestions for ways that the journal session can be entered to maximize safety and comfort. Mark the ones that appeal to you; then add your own.

- Have a quiet room or place to write in
- Lots of privacy
- Light a candle
- Write or say a prayer before I get started asking for help and guidance
- Set aside enough time so that I can get in and out of the work without feeling rushed
- Be somewhere <u>other</u> than my room; keeping my room a safe place
- Stay focused — jotting down random or extraneous thoughts in the margins of my journal so I don't distract myself but still can come back to things that might be worth looking at later
- (If you smoke) have cigarettes, matches, and a clean ashtray
- Make a pot of coffee or tea
- Play the right "mood music" on the stereo or CD player
- Perform stretching or deep breathing ahead of time to get my energy moving
- Write in my journal before a therapy session so I know I've got support for what comes up
- Arrange to have other people around in case I need help
- Write affirmations on 3x5 cards and have them handy
- Limit the length of time I write so I don't get lost or overwhelmed
- Give myself permission to quit any time I want to, even if I'm not finished
- Play a tape of nature sounds (birdsongs, waterfalls, oceans, thunderstorms)
- Write a focusing statement or Springboard so I can stay on track
- Have plenty of paper in my notebook
- Try out the pen before I start to make sure it's comfortable to write with
- Put on soothing music with headphones to screen out background noise
- Warm up with drawing or sketching
- Spiritually center myself before I start
- Put the answering machine on; hang a "Do Not Disturb" sign on my door
- Draw an angel card before I start and warm up by writing how the angel can help me

From *The Way of the Journal,* © Kathleen Adams (1998, Sidran Press)   6

In the space below, write additional ways in which **you** can feel safe, comfortable and nurtured while you do process journal work:

Rewarding Yourself When It's Over

In addition to empowering yourself at the beginning of a journal session by creating a nurturing, safe, comfortable environment, it is equally important to empower yourself at the end of the session by exiting gracefully and rewarding yourself for doing work that is sometimes painful and difficult. Here are some ideas of an "aprés-journal" treat from journal group participants. Check the ones you like, and add your own goodies to the list.

- Take a bubble bath
- Go for a walk or run
- Breathe fresh air
- Listen to music
- Change the music from whatever's been on in background while I've been writing
- Read a good book
- Call a friend
- Play a tape of nature sounds
- Tell somebody what I just did and ask for acknowledgment
- Ask for a hug
- Give myself positive strokes
- Do something active
- Put on dance music and boogie
- Lie down
- Stretch and breathe
- Bake cookies
- Find someone who's willing to listen while I read what I've just written
- Watch soap operas or junk television
- Play the piano and sing
- Blow out the candle
- Put my journal away

Add yours here:

A Contract With Myself

I, _____, am committed to using my journal as a
(Write your name here)

tool for personal growth, psychological healing, emotional recovery and empowerment. I

will use my journal responsibly by learning different ways to utilize it and by making my

environment safe, comfortable and nurturing. I will especially remember to create a con-

ducive environment for journalkeeping by doing the following things before I begin to

write:

When I am finished, I will reward myself for my efforts by

I thank myself for doing this work.

_____

(Sign your name here)

_____

(Put today's date here)

From *The Way of the Journal,* © Kathleen Adams (1998, Sidran Press)

Structure,
Containment,
Pacing:
Three Vital Journal
Tools

Building Structure in Your Journal

• Use structured techniques that have well-defined boundaries and clearly sequenced tasks. Examples:
  • The 5-Minute Sprint has a **time limit.**
  • Clustering has **physical boundaries.**
  • The Structured Writing Exercise has **sequenced tasks.**
  • Lists have **boundaries** and **end limits.**
  • Sentence Stems have **end limits.**
• Use structure in your environment. Find out what "props" you like to have in place (peppermint tea, special music, your cat in your lap) and arrange for them. Know what works for you. Use your entry/exit checklists. Create writing rituals that soothe or empower you.
• If you are having intrusive thoughts or auditory or visual hallucinations, writing may not be too helpful. You run the risk of further disorganization and exacerbating a sense of helplessness. If you do decide to write in this state, please give yourself permission to stop when you need to.
• Lined paper helps you feel structured. If you don't know your preference between wide and narrow lines, find out.

Building Containment in Your Journal

• Use your journal book literally as a container. Know that when you write, you are moving thoughts/feelings/energy OUT of your mind and body and INTO a neutral, receptive place where they will be stored safely for you. The easiest journal containment skills are:
  • Close the book and
  • Put it away.
• If you have written something you don't want to reread without assistance, **fold the pages in** to alert you to proceed with caution. This also lets your therapist turn right to those pages.
• Use the page margins as boundaries.
• Contain the time or amount of your writing, such as:
  • Write for 15 minutes and stop.
  • Write for two pages and stop.
• Clustering is a good "container" technique because it *looks* like a container on the page.

Building Pacing in Your Journal

• Be a dolphin. Dive deep and surface. Go into the heart of the issue, then come sharply to the surface, look around, grab some air, go back into the heart. Do this many times, even when you don't need to, for practice.
• Write the word BREATHE at the top of every journal page. Any time you glance at that word, stop where you are and take a deep breath.

• Write a statement of your intention at the beginning of a journal session. When you come to the surface, flip back to the statement of intention and review it. Check to see if you're still on track.

• Write three feeling words at the beginning and the end of your journal entry.

• STOP when you sense yourself becoming overwhelmed. Use common sense. It is unhealthy to ignore your own warning signs.

• Use a foreground/background exercise such as *Now I am aware of . . . And that reminds me of . . .* to shuttle back and forth between present and past.

• Move. Move around. Get up and stretch, walk, get a drink. Then come back to your journal.

*Eight Suggestions
For Satisfying
Journal Writing*

1. **Start with an entrance meditation.** Just about every technique benefits from a few minutes of focused quieting at the beginning. Use visualization, soft music, candles, deep breathing, yoga stretches, whatever works for you. Quiet your head chatter and focus on the technique or topic you've chosen.

2. **Date every entry.** If you only establish one habit in your journal, let it be this one. Dating every entry allows you to chronologically reconstruct your journal by date. It also gives you the opportunity to observe cycles, patterns and trends. Over time, you'll begin to notice and plan for your down times, your creative times, your introspective times.

3. **Keep what you write.** Often the stuff that feels like junk contains the seeds for future insight ("journal kernels"!). You'll often find that you'll write something that appears to make no sense or has little relevance, only to come across it days, weeks or months later and find that it's exactly what you need to read!

4. **Write quickly.** You can outsmart dreaded "writer's block" by writing so fast that the Internal Critic and the Internal Censor can't catch up. Writing quickly also provides more ready access to subconscious information, because you're not as liable to consciously think about what you're writing.

5. **Start writing; keep writing.** Begin. Just begin. Put pen to paper and begin to write. Once you've started, keep going. And don't go back and "fix" your glitches; they're often your subconscious mind's way of hollering for your attention. Let your Freudians slip!

6. **Tell the complete truth faster.** Don't try to snooker yourself into not knowing what you know. You'll get the best results in your journal if you give yourself permission to go to the bottom line, even if it sounds ugly, awful, scary or negative.

7. **Protect your own privacy.** Get in the habit of storing your journal in its own special place so that the temptation for others to read is diminished. Reserve the first page of any new journal for your name, address and phone number, along with a disclaimer: *This is my personal journal. Please don't read it without my knowledge and permission.* Or you can be more direct: *KEEP OUT!* A nice, firm compromise: *Thank you for respecting my privacy.*

8. **Write naturally.** If there is one inviolate rule of journal writing, it is that there simply *are no rules!* Writing naturally means that you do what works for you and don't worry about what you're *not* doing in the journal. Writing naturally means that you

Adapted from *Journal to the Self* (1980, Warner Books) and *The Way of the Journal,* © Kathleen Adams (1993, Sidran Press)   12

pick your journal up when the mood strikes and put it down when the mood shifts; that you allow for changes in focus, penmanship, point of view. Writing naturally means that you give yourself permission to use your journal as a blank canvas onto which the rich and intricate portrait of your life can be painted as it naturally emerges. There is only *one* person who can write the story of your life. Writing naturally means that you let yourself be *you*.

Adapted from *Journal to the Self* (1980, Warner Books) and *The Way of the Journal*, © Kathleen Adams (1993, Sidran Press)

STOP!

This is the personal journal of

Do not read any further unless you have been given permission.

Journals Quick & Easy

Here's the shortest, most highly structured, most contained journal technique of all: Sentence Stems. Fill in the blank with one word or phrase, and you're done.

It doesn't get any quicker or easier!

Turn the page and complete the Sentence Stems. When you're finished, come back to this page and reflect in the section titled **So, how was it?**

Day One:
Sentence Stems

Today's Date:

_____

So, how was it?
What do you like/not like about Sentence Stems? What did you learn about yourself? When might you use this technique?

_____

Closing thoughts . . .
What's the weather like? What does it remind me of?

Sentence Stems

Complete these sentences with the first word that comes to mind. Try not to censor or judge.

A word that describes me is ....

A word that describes my journal is ....

When I check inside, I find ....

My Inner Critic says I'm ....

My Inner Wisdom says I'm ....

The person I feel closest to is ....

If my present mood were a color, it would be ....

Complete these Sentence Stems with a longer thought. Again, try not to edit your thoughts.

I am a person who

If I had time I would

I am grateful for

Journal writing is

Complete these Sentence Stems at least three different ways.

When I think about writing a journal, I . . .

-
-
-

The most important things to do right now are . . .

-
-
-

I want . . .

-
-
-

The biggest challenges I am facing now are . . .

-
-
-

Write your own Sentence Stems here. Complete them several different ways.

Day Two:
The 5-Minute
Writing Sprint

━━━━━━━━━━

Today's Date:

Even people who don't have time can find 5-minute pockets throughout the day. On telephone hold, in a traffic jam, in a waiting room, in the bathtub, on your coffee break, first thing in the morning, last thing at night. Keep your journal with you, and start mastering the art of the 5-Minute Sprint.

On the next page you'll read more about the 5-Minute Sprint. The following pages are blank for your own writing sprints. When you're finished, come back and reflect.

_____

So, how was it?
What do you like/not like about the 5-Minute Sprints? What did you learn about yourself? When might you use this technique?

_____

By the way. . .
What was the worst thing that happened to me today? What was the best?

WHEN? The 5-Minute Sprint is useful when—
- you're overwhelmed
- you don't have much time
- you don't know what to write about
- you have a lot going on
- you need clarity and focus
- you really don't want to write
- you want to track an issue/feeling/project over time

HOW? It's easy! All you do is—
- pick a subject
- write as fast as you can
- at the end of five minutes, STOP
- re-read what you've written
- continue if you want — or put your journal aside!

WHAT? Try using the 5-Minute Writing Sprint to write about—
- what's going on
- the present moment
- a person or relationship
- your therapy session or support group meeting
- a feeling or mood
- something silly or irrelevant
- background ("wallpaper") issues
- a decision or choice
- a check-in with yourself
- Best Thing/Worst Thing of your day/present moment
- an insight, awareness or "aha"
- last night's dream
- a Cluster you've just done
- something you don't want to forget
- your goals for the day
- a Captured Moment
- things that are going right; things that are going wrong
- an AlphaPoem or other creative writing
- something upsetting
- YOU NAME IT! You can write for 5 minutes about anything!

TIPS:
- if you have a timer handy (on your watch or in the kitchen, for instance), set it for 5 minutes.
- if not, note the time at the start of your entry.
- **IMPORTANT:** STOP when you told yourself you would!
- you can always write more!
- ease into writing about trauma- or shame-based issues with Sprints.
- there's nothing magical about 5 minutes other than most people agree they can find 5 minutes. If it's frustratingly short, try 10-Minute Sprints.

Write your own 5-Minute Sprint on this page.   Suggestions:
- How do you feel about writing a journal?
- What's going on for you *right now,* in this moment?
- Review your day from the time you opened your eyes this morning.
- Name a feeling you're having right now and explore it.

Day Three:
The Structured
Writing Exercise

Today we'll expand yesterday's short, simple structure into a longer, more complex structure. Another timed writing, but one with more pieces. **Do them all, in order!**

Something very powerful goes on in this exercise. Check it out.

Today's Date:

So, how was it?
What do you like/not like about the Structured Writing Exercise? What did you learn about yourself? When might you use this technique?

I almost forgot . . .
Have I laughed today? When, where and why?

Useful when:
- you don't know how to start
- you don't want to get overwhelmed
- you want to focus on one area
- you want to track an issue over time
- you want to "contain" material

STEP ONE:

Notice the **time**. This is a **timed** writing process of 15-20 minutes.

STEP TWO:

Write the date, time and **three feeling words** at the top of your page. The three feeling words should answer the question: "How do I feel **right now?**"

STEP THREE:

Close your eyes and take **ten** slow, deep inhale/exhale breaths. This takes 60-90 seconds. Concentrate on your breathing. Allow any tension or pain in your body to dissipate on the exhale breaths.

STEP FOUR:

Take one or two minutes to focus on your topic. If you don't know it in advance, let yourself "intuit" what you want or need to write about. Finish the Sentence Stem, *I want to explore* . . . .

STEP FIVE:

Explore the Sentence Stem using the following format:
- The first thing that comes to mind . . .
- Beneath the surface I find . . .
- What feels uncomfortable or disturbs me about this is . . .
- What gives me hope or inspires me about this is . . .
- I would benefit from . . .
- My next step is to . . .

Write for 10 minutes (about two sentences each).

STEP SIX:

Review (re-read) what you have written. "Sit" with it a minute. Jot down any awarenesses, insights, thoughts you have about what you've written.

STEP SEVEN:

Write three feeling words at the bottom of your entry.

Write your own Structured Write here. Because there is so much structure, pacing and containment built into the process, you might want to choose a topic or issue that's fairly "loaded" for you.

Day Four:
Clustering

Today's Date:

Here's another quick and easy technique with the potential for startling results. Clustering combines the intuitive aspects of free-association with just enough structure to organize and make connections.

This exercise isn't timed, but you'll likely generate your Cluster in less than 10 minutes. Do a 5-Minute Sprint to synthesize the ideas in the Cluster, then come back to this page and reflect.

Try Clustering your day just before you go to bed by using today's date as the central Cluster point. It's a great way to gather up the loose thoughts and events of the day and braid them together so they're not roaming around in your head as you try to fall asleep.

So, how was it?
What do you like/not like about Clustering? What did you learn about yourself? When might you use this technique?

In other news . . .
What's in foreground for me today?

Why Cluster?

> quick and easy
> Generates ideas and insights
> Breaks through internal barriers
> Provides details of inner organization and history
> Good for getting unstuck
> Helps with communication and understanding of other
> persons, parts of yourself, issues, feelings

Choose a word or phrase as a topic: a mood, issue, person, memory, part of yourself, feeling, dream symbol or character, today's date. Write this in the center of the page and circle it. Turn off all internal censors and judgments. What's the first thing that comes to mind? Write this above, below, or to the side of your cluster word, circle it, and draw a line connecting it to the middle. What does the second word make you think of? Write it down, circle it, connect it with a line to the word before it. Continue in this way until you can go no further.

Now return to the original word and begin the process again, spinning a new thought-line of associations that occur spontaneously. You can go back to previous thought-lines at any time and add in more assocations. Soon your page will begin to look like a web of concentric rings. You'll know you're done when you run out of juice (or paper!) or when you feel a slight internal shift. Stop, survey your Cluster, let associations come together in your mind, and write a 5-Minute Sprint that synthesizes your discoveries or expands on one area of the Cluster.

With each Cluster you'll find a *personal expanded definition* of the theme that represents a personal history of your relationship to it. It is, therefore, a way of better understanding your meaning when you use the Cluster word or phrase.

Clustering does not have to lead to detailed and complex analysis. Often the pattern becomes apparent upon first view. If you don't have time or energy to write a detailed entry, try Clustering instead!

Example:

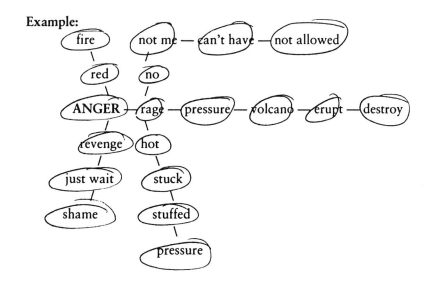

---

[2]Thanks to Bruce Brooks, M.Div. for some of these interpretations of the Clustering technique.

From *The Way of the Journal,* © Kathleen Adams (1998, Sidran Press)   27

Use this page for your own Cluster. On the following page, write a 5-Minute Sprint exploring some aspect of the Clustering process. Suggestions for your Cluster:

- a feeling you have difficulty with
- a quality you'd like more of
- some project from your "to-do" list

Synthesize your Cluster here.

Day Five:
AlphaPoems

A perennial journal group favorite, this simple poetic device is so effective that even staunch "non-poets" beg to read their poems aloud.

Variations on the theme: Instead of using the entire alphabet, write a key word (an emotion, a name, a therapeutic issue) vertically down your page and structure your AlphaPoem around it:

Today's Date:

Just two
Ordinary people — but with
You, I feel alive.

So, how was it?
What do you like/not like about AlphaPoems? What did you learn about yourself? When might you use this technique?

Before I forget . . .
Whom do I feel close to? Why?

Try this creative, fun and astonishingly "write on" idea for checking in with yourself: AlphaPoems!

STEP #1: Pick a subject. Any subject. For starters:
• a feeling (e.g., anger, shame, grief, regret, joy, pain)
• a mood (e.g., grouchy, depressed, happy, excited, chaotic)
• a subpersonality (e.g., the Critic, the Overachiever, the Wise One)
• a task (e.g., things to do today, a project)
• a person in your life (e.g., friend, partner, child, parent, therapist, roommate)
• a therapeutic issue (e.g., an addiction, a relationship, a healing)
• what's going on (a sure-fire way to find out!)

STEP #2: Write a poem about your subject in which each successive line begins with the next letter of the alphabet. (Perfectly acceptable to use Xceptions for Xtra-hard letters!) Work quickly to maximize creativity and unexpected results.

An AlphaPoem On AlphaPoems

Anticipate a
Blossoming of
Creative
Delight!
Effortless, really, once you
Find the rhythm and the pace.
Gather up the thoughts you hold secret in your
Heart.
Imagine them
Just drifting out, a
Kaleidoscope of
Letters
Making words.
No "rules" to follow (except the
Obvious one.) Perhaps you'll find a
Poet inside?
Quite likely!
Re-read your AlphaPoems; you'll find them
Startlingly
True — an
Unusual way to give
Voice to the
Wails, wonderings, whimpers, whys, wins.
Xhilarating feeling to find
You've reached the
Zenith of the poem!

31

Try an AlphaPoem here. Call it What's Going On?

What's Going On?

A

B

C

D

E

F

G

H

I

J

K

L

M

N

O

P

Q

R

S

T

U

V

W

X

Y

Z

Day Six: Character Sketch

Today's Date:

A Character Sketch is a written portrait of another person or a part of yourself. When you write about another — especially someone you're scared of, having difficulty with, or admire greatly — it's an excellent opportunity to tune into your *projections* (those unknown or disowned parts of yourself that you "see" in other people).

You can also come to know more about your feelings and emotions by personifying them as people, animals or other animate objects and writing Character Sketches of them.

Character Sketches of your friends, family, children, co-workers make great greeting-card entries for birthdays, holidays, special occasions!

So, how was it?
What do you like/not like about Character Sketch? What did you learn about yourself? When might you use this technique?

I was just thinking . . .
If I could change one habit, what would it be?

Character Sketch

A Character Sketch is a written description of a person or part of yourself. It's a useful journal tool to use to help you **identify projections, gather information** and **get to know different parts of yourself.**

You may write Character Sketches . . .

- of people you admire or respond well to, to help you identify qualities you can use for positive role modeling

- of people who make you angry or who upset you in some way, to help you identify any projections you may be making

- of your "subpersonalities" (the different parts of yourself, such as your Wounded Child, Inner Critic, Inner Wisdom, Perfectionist, Nurturer, etc.), to help you find out how you can best access their messages, wisdom and/or assistance

- of your friends, to share your feelings and connect in a meaningful way

- of yourself, from the point of view of another (your spouse, best friend, boss, etc.), to see how you might be coming across to someone else

There's no "right" or "wrong" way to write a Character Sketch . . . but here are some points you may want to consider:

- Begin by closing your eyes and imagining this person, part of yourself, etc. What do you notice first? Physical qualities? Feelings? Their "essence"?

- Tune in to questions like . . . What are this person's likes and dislikes? What is important to him/her? How do you feel about this person? What does s/he need/want/fear? What do you and this person have as points of agreement/disagreement? What "bugs" you about this person? What is the purpose of this person's life? What is this person's role? Function? What do you imagine this person would say if s/he could make a statement about the world and her/his role in it?

- If you're having a hard time getting started, try **Clustering** with the person's name in the middle of the page. Your Character Sketch can often be written directly from the information gathered in the Cluster.

- Or try just writing a Character Sketch in the form of a **List** of qualities, attributes, your feelings about the person, etc.

- Character Sketches frequently shift into journal **Dialogues.**

From *The Way of the Journal,* © Kathleen Adams (1998, Sidran Press)   35

Write a Character Sketch. Suggestions:

• someone you admire and would like to emulate
• someone who scares or intimidates you
• close your eyes and imagine a feeling as if it were a person

Day Seven:
Dialogue

Today's Date:

Here's another tried-and-true journal favorite. On the page, a journal Dialogue looks like a movie or play script:

Me: You're all very small.
Fears: Fears don't grow, they multiply.

Don't worry if it feels like you're making it up. You *are* making it up! After you get the rhythm going, though, you'll likely forget to feel foolish . . . and the results can be truly remarkable.

Give yourself at least 20 minutes for a Dialogue. After you've practiced a few times, you may want to set aside as much as an hour for a Dialogue journal session.

So, how was it?

What do you like/not like about the Dialogue technique? What did you learn about yourself? When might you use this technique?

Now that you mention it . . .
What's the most important thing to do?

The Dialogue technique is the Swiss Army Knife of the journal toolbox. A marvel of flexibility, Dialogue can take you into or through nearly any journal situation you can imagine. It is the technique of choice of many experienced journal writers.

There are many types of Dialogues, some of which come from Dr. Ira Progoff's Intensive Journal™ Workshop:

- **Dialogue with Persons.** This Dialogue can be with anyone in your life — past, present or future; living, dead or not yet born. The person you choose to dialogue with does not need to be someone you actually know.
- **Dialogue with Works.** Dialogue with your present job, your fantasy job, your career to date, your hobbies or leisure-time activities, your creative works, the Muse, your Life's Work.
- **Dialogue with the Body.** The innate wisdom of the body speaks in often direct metaphor, and a written dialogue enables you to find out what your body is trying to teach you. Try a dialogue with a body part or organ; an illness, injury or surgery; an addiction or habit; allergies; sexuality; body subpersonalities (Thin Self, Fat Self, The Addict); foods and nutrition; pain (always a messenger!)

Other Dialogues can serve you as you explore your treatment issues:

- **Dialogue with Emotions/Feelings.** The feelings you have rarely or never allowed yourself to experience can be mystifying; sometimes it's hard to even put a name on them. Let the Dialogue serve as a reality check.
- **Dialogue with Symbols.** Dream characters and symbols help you learn more about the various dimensions of your life that they represent. Give them a "voice."
- **Dialogue with Memories.** Sometimes "objectifying" a memory and treating it like a dialogue partner helps you gain useful distance and clarity.
- **Dialogue with Resistance/Block.** When you're stuck, acknowledge it and work with it. The way out is through. Close your eyes and create a mental picture of the stuckness, resistance or block. Then dialogue with it.
- **Dialogue with Your Therapist or Teacher.** Especially helpful when you're feeling overwhelmed, out of control or unable to manage impulses. Write a journal Dialogue with your therapist or a key teacher in your life in which you allow yourself to remember the support and guidance you'd receive if you were in an actual conversation.

In a class by itself is Progoff's:

- **Dialogue with Inner Wisdom.** "Man does indeed know intuitively more than he rationally understands," writes Progoff, and the Inner Wisdom Dialogue allows you to give voice to the part of you that knows your Truth. Dialoguing with God, your Higher Power, your Internal Self-Helper, or any other expression of your inner wisdom can be a beautiful, spiritual, lyrical experience.

Any time you are writing a journal Dialogue, remember:
- Each party to the Dialogue may ask any question and receive an honest answer
- Each party may make any statement or express any opinion and know it will be heard

Adapted from *Journal to the Self* (1980, Warner Books) and *The Way of the Journal,* © Kathleen Adams (1993, Sidran Press)   38

Suggestions For Satisfying Journal Dialogue

- Create a pleasant environment. Make sure you have the privacy and space you need. Do whatever you need to ensure your optimum comfort.

- Give yourself time. The most effective Dialogues tend to unfold in cycles or waves of writing and reflection.

- Start with an entrance meditation. Reflect on the relationship you currently have with your Dialogue partner, how the relationship feels to you, any questions you'd like to ask, any statements you'd like to make.

- Warm up with other techniques. Try a Character Sketch of your Dialogue partner, or a list of questions you'd like to ask. If you are dialoguing with an abstraction, personify your Dialogue partner in some way. This makes conversing easier, and it also allows a "relationship of equals" (Progoff).

- Allow yourself to feel uncomfortable. It is perfectly natural to feel as if you are making it up and to feel silly or awkward until you get the hang of the Dialogue technique.

- Respect the silence. Sometimes you'll come to a stopping place, where the words or thoughts or images seem to dry up. When you come to a natural pause, close your eyes and wait in silence for the next question or answer. It is sometimes helpful to quietly ask yourself, "What does my heart say?" Re-reading what you have written will often allow the Dialogue to spontaneously resume.

- Exit gracefully. If the Dialogue does not resume after sitting in silence and/or re-reading, you may be approaching completion. Ask in the Dialogue itself: "Is there anything else?" It's a nice touch to thank your Dialogue partner and ask permission to contact him/her/it again for another conversation.

- Have fun. Some of your Dialogue partners will take on quirky "personalities" that can range from annoying to amusing. Expecting the unexpected is a delightful part of the Dialogue process.

- Trust the process. You may get answers and insights that seem to come from nowhere. The Dialogue technique is a way of bringing information from the unconscious mind into consciousness, where it may feel foreign, unfamiliar, or unsettling. Trust the process. Trust the process. Trust. Trust. Trust.

Try a journal Dialogue with the subject of Day Six's Character Sketch. Dialogues often take off in directions you wouldn't have expected, so extra pages are included.

Continue your Dialogue here . . . or start a new one!

Dialogue, continued . . .

Day Eight:
Springboards

Today's Date:

Springboards give you a jumping-off place . . . a "topic sentence" for your journal entry. As a very general rule, Springboards phrased as a **question** (What do I want?) will generate more feeling responses, and Springboards phrased as a **sentence stem** (I want . . .) will generate more thinking responses.

Make a list of Springboards (points from groups or therapy sessions, ideas to ponder, "aha"s that come to you at random) on the inside back cover of your journal. Then you'll always have something to write about when you don't know what to write about!

For now, choose one or two of the questions from the list on the next page. Try a 5-Minute Sprint (Day Two), or a Structured Write (Day Three). Or, just free-write!

_____

So, how was it?
What do you like/not like about Springboards? What did you learn about yourself? When might you use this technique?

_____

What I really want to know is . . .
What do I want?

If you never did anything in your journal but answer these three Springboards, you'd run through a lot of notebooks, because the answers change constantly.

- **Who am I?**
  Who am I today?
  Who was I yesterday?
  Who am I becoming?
  What is my identity?
  What names am I known by?
  What parts of myself do I reveal to others?
  What parts do I conceal?
  Who have I been in the past?
  What roles or masks have I discarded?
  Who is my authentic self?
  With whom do I share my true self?

- **Why am I here?**
  What is my purpose for being in this place right now?
  What do I have to learn?
  What do I have to teach?
  What experiences in my recent past have prepared me to be here?
  How did I get here?
  Do I want to stay here?
  Where do I want to go next?
  What does this present moment offer me?
  What do I bring to the present moment?

- **What do I want?**
  What do I want for myself?
  What do I want for others?
  What do I want for the world?
  What do I want to do?
  What do I want to be?
  What do I want to have?
  What is the most important thing to do?
  What do I need to have?
  What do I need to know?
  What do I need to do?
  Do I have what I want?
  Do I want what I have?

These questions are a lifetime's study. Don't tackle them all at once, and don't expect yourself to know the answers! You *can* expect greater clarity and increased awareness as you address these questions in your journal. You can also expect more questions!

Remember that flipping the question around into a Sentence Stem might offer more logical, cognitive responses. This isn't a hard-and-fast rule, but it's worth checking out for yourself.

Choose one of the Springboard questions from the prior page and write until you feel you're done.

Continue your Springboard exploration here . . . or start a new one!

Day Nine:
Poetry

Forget all the reasons you think you can't write poetry. In your journal, anything goes! There are times when trying to make orderly sense out of language just doesn't work. So when you find yourself unable to articulate, forget form and structure and try a poem.

Today's Date:

So, how was it?
What do you like/not like about writing poetry? What did you learn about yourself? When might you use this technique again?

Funny you should ask . . .
How can I set free the poet inside me?

Here's How To Write
A Poem

Here's how to write a poem.
Just start somewhere
   (anywhere)
with a thought
   or an image
   or a question
   or a feeling
   or a phrase that strikes your fancy.
Or pick a theme
   I remember . . .
   I'm wishing . . .
Repeat throughout. Place it as the title
   like a crown.
Cluster a poem
   spinning webs,
   weaving images.
Stuck? Write the last line
   (**any** last line)
near the bottom of the page — then fill the
     s p a c e in between.
Poems may rhyme; they may keep time. And they may not.
Here's a tip: Write "normally"
then find the natural rhythm of your words.
Like artist with paintbrush in hand
   break a line
   add a stroke
   rearrange
Voila! You've painted a poem!

ON WRITING A POEM

Sometimes I write the endings first
and middles find themselves in stockinged feet
awakened, yawning, from a slumbering state
and called to active duty,
   unprepared.

The writing life has many joys
among them flexibility of form.
An icy mountain stream of words
in gentle chaos tumbling forth,
creating right relationship:
an image midwifed to its natural birth,
a ripely flowered seed pod
full of dreams.

From *The Way of the Journal*, © Kathleen Adams (1998, Sidran Press)   48

Try your hand at poetry here. Tips for getting started:

• think of a phrase, or borrow one from another poem, to use as a repeating phrase throughout.
• use a scene or event in nature as a metaphor for something in your life
• make word pictures out of an experience from your day
• write a poem about or to someone you love

Poet Linda Pastan says she rewrites each poem at least 100 times. So don't feel bad if you've scratched out!

Day Ten:
Free Writing

Today's Date:

Congratulations! You've come to the end of the Journals Quick and Easy 10-Day Journal Jump-Start Program! You've learned lots of different ways to write in your journal. Some of them no doubt appeal to you more than others. That's fine. As you come to befriend your journal, you'll find yourself drawn to certain techniques for certain purposes . . . but the others are there waiting for you, when the time and subject are right.

The last technique you'll learn in this workbook is **Free Writing.** As the name implies, it's unstructured, free-form narrative writing that starts anywhere and goes where it pleases.

Begin by just beginning. Without much planning or forethought, just let yourself get started. Write down the next thing in your mind. After a few minutes, your thoughts may begin to clarify and your feelings may start to crystallize. Free writing is like body surfing. Ride the waves wherever they take you, but know your own signals. If you start to feel like you're out too far or under too deep, drop back to a lower rung on the structure/pacing/containment ladder.

So, how was it?
What do you like/not like about Free Writing? What did you learn about yourself? When might you use this technique?

Closing thoughts . . .
What's my next step?

Start with your present moment. How do you feel right now? What are you aware of right now? What do you want to say?

Continued . . .

Graduation:
Journal Dialogue

Today's Date:

How are you feeling about your journal? Different from when you began this workbook? I hope you're beginning to develop a *relationship* with your journal just like you develop relationships with your friends, colleagues, therapist, and other important people in your life.

On the following pages, write a Dialogue with your journal. Then — you know the routine — come back and reflect one last time.

So, how was it?
What did you like/not like about writing a dialogue with your journal? What did you learn about yourself? When might you use this technique?

Goodbye for now . . .
How do I handle goodbyes?

Feelings & Imagery

A Baker's Dozen Journal Things To Do With Feelings

1. Write a Character Sketch of a feeling. Describe it as a person, animal or other living object. Visualize its dress, age, physical presence, emotional wants and needs, message to the world, how it got that way, when you first became acquainted, etc.

2. Cluster your feeling to better understand your personal history and associations to the feeling.

3. Write an AlphaPoem about the feeling, using either the entire alphabet or the letters of the feeling.

4. Dialogue with the feeling. Give it a voice. (Great to do after a Character Sketch of a feeling.)

5. Write the Stepping Stones (major turning points) of your emotional life, from birth to the present moment.

6. Make a list of the feelings you know well, recognize instantly and hang out with regularly. Make another list of all the feelings you only are acquainted with. Make a third list of feelings that you don't relate to or understand.

7. Use the sentence completion Feelings Worksheet (see next page) to explore any of your feelings.

8. Each night before you go to bed, decide on a feeling you'd like to experience the next day. Write this feeling in your journal as the "emotion du jour." As you go to sleep, think about the feeling you've chosen. How would you recognize it? What would you be doing? How would your physical body reflect this feeling (laughing, open body posture, quiet, making eye contact, etc.)? Who could "reality check" you about this feeling? Each night, write a 5-Minute Sprint using the Springboard, "How did I experience (feeling) today?"

9. Write a love letter — to yourself, or to someone you care about, or to someone who is no longer in your life.

10. Write a haiku (three-line poem of five, seven, five syllables) that crystallizes your feeling into one potent image.

11. Write a Stream of Consciousness/Free Writing entry using your feeling word as a starting place.

12. Think of an image or metaphor that represents your feeling and use it as the organizing theme of a poem.

13. Represent your feeling in art — drawing, painting, collage. Use color and shape if form does not come easily for you. Or find a picture in a magazine that represents your feeling and paste or tape it in your journal. Write about the picture.

From *The Way of the Journal,* © Kathleen Adams (1998, Sidran Press)   57

Feelings Worksheet

The feeling I wish to work with is

....

If this feeling had a color, it would be

....

If this feeling had a shape, it would be

....

If this feeling had a texture, it would be

....

If this feeling had a temperature, it would be

....

If this feeling had a size, it would be

....

If this feeling were a weather condition, it would be

....

The place in my body where this feeling hangs out is

....

If this feeling could talk, it would say

....

And it would also say

....

What I want to say back to this feeling is

....

Three instances when I distinctly remember having this feeling are

1) ....

2) ....

3) ....

Usually when I have this feeling I

....

Or else I

The way I deal with this feeling is

And I also

The way I could use this feeling productively is

And I could also

I block myself from knowing more about this feeling because

I'm afraid that if I let myself truly feel this feeling, I would

And that would mean

But what I really want is

And

The three things I'm willing to do, **starting now,** to change my relationship to this feeling are

1)

2)

3)

I will ask for support from

Feelings Worksheet

The feeling I wish to work with is

....

If this feeling had a color, it would be

....

If this feeling had a shape, it would be

....

If this feeling had a texture, it would be

....

If this feeling had a temperature, it would be

....

If this feeling had a size, it would be

....

If this feeling were a weather condition, it would be

....

The place in my body where this feeling hangs out is

....

If this feeling could talk, it would say

....

And it would also say

....

What I want to say back to this feeling is

....

Three instances when I distinctly remember having this feeling are

1) ....

2) ....

3) ....

Usually when I have this feeling I

....

Or else I

The way I deal with this feeling is

And I also

The way I could use this feeling productively is

And I could also

I block myself from knowing more about this feeling because

I'm afraid that if I let myself truly feel this feeling, I would

And that would mean

But what I really want is

And

The three things I'm willing to do, **starting now,** to change my relationship to this feeling are

1)

2)

3)

I will ask for support from

*A Baker's Dozen
Journal Things To
Do With Dreams*

1. Record your dream upon awakening. Use the present tense to add immediacy and to honor the dream's ongoing life force. Don't remember the entire dream? Record scenes, fragments, snatches, even impressions. When it comes to dreamwork in your journal, a little can go a long way.

2. Name your dreams as you would a short story or painting or poem. Keep a separate, running list of your dream titles somewhere in your journal. Themes will often jump out at you.

3. If you don't remember your dreams, try writing a note to your "Dreamkeeper" in your journal before you turn out the lights. It might be as simple as, "Dear Dreamkeeper, Please bring me a dream that I'll remember tomorrow morning. I promise I'll write it down and pay attention to it. Thanks!"

4. After you've recorded your dream, write a Five- or Ten-Minute Sprint in which you give your best guess as to what this dream might be saying about your waking life.

5. Write a list of questions raised by the dream. Leave yourself a few lines between questions. Then go back and answer the questions. Do this quickly and without much conscious thought.

6. Cluster your dream symbols.

7. Dialogue with your dream characters.

8. Free Write about a particularly elusive symbol or character.

9. Write a Captured Moment of a scene from the dream, focusing on the sensory details.

10. Shift perspectives. Take a key symbol or character from your dream, and rewrite the dream as if that symbol or character were the dreamer. Or let the symbol/character interpret itself, by writing in the first person from its perspective ("I am the winding dirt road. I am in this dream because.....").

11. Play Western Union. Rewrite the dream using as few words as possible, in telegram style.

12. Write a poem about the dream. Focus on the images and feelings. Try an Alphapoem about a dream symbol, scene or character.

13. Paint, draw or sketch the dream or its symbols.

Dream Worksheet

(Make photocopies of these pages to work with, or follow these steps in your journal.)

Today's Date _____

Dream Title _____
       (see below)

Synopsis of the dream, written in *present tense* to give immediacy to the dream. Include as much detail as you can. Don't overlook seemingly "throw-away" symbols or details.

(cont. on back, if needed)

What is the name of this dream? Give it a title in the box below.

<table><tr><td>

</td></tr></table>

(continued . . .)

What was the predominant feeling tone of this dream?

If you awakened with any sensation or feeling in your body, note it here.

In the left column, list the primary symbols, characters and actions of the dream. On the back, or on a separate page, cluster (see Day Four) with the dream elements until you get a "best guess" of what each might mean. In the right column, list your best guesses.

Dream Element   Best Guess

(continued . . .)

What is your best guess about what this dream might be trying to tell you?

Action steps suggested:

Thank you, Dreamkeeper, for the lessons in this dream!

Using Imagery For
Safety And Protection

In mythological times, heroes and heroines had advisors (sometimes from the animal or bird kingdoms), shields, lanterns and talismans to help them stay safe and protected on their journeys. In this journal process, we will create a series of safety and protection images that you can use when you do painful or difficult work in your journal. We will create a guide, a shield, a light source, and a bridge back to the present.

Don't fill out this part yet. This is a summary of the next few pages. Complete it after you have finished the exercise!*

My guide is

....

I use it to

....

My shield is

....

I use it to

....

My light source is

....

I use it to

....

....

My bridge back to the present is

....

I use it to

....

....

....

It's always nice to have a wise, caring companion when you're embarking on a difficult journey. Think about the qualities you'd like to have in a companion if you were undertaking a mythological adventure. You might want someone who, or something that:
- knows the way
- has travelled this road before
- has the gift of insight or intuition
- has a sense of humor
- has enough courage for both of you

(now fill in your own)

....

....

....

Your guide can be a man or a woman (or genderless), an adult or a child (or a youth), a bird or an animal (or a fish!). He/she/it can be old or young, big or small, talkative or quiet, Chinese or Indian or Italian or Jewish, practical or mystical. If you were making up a guide to take with you on your journal journeys (which is exactly what you're doing), what qualities would you want your guide to have? List them here.

My guide would be ....

And my guide would be ....

And ....

And my guide would be ....

Give your guide a name ....
Now close your eyes and imagine this guide. See if you can picture yourself standing before or beside your guide. Check out all the characteristics you've just listed above.

How are you going to access your guide before you start your journal entry? You might:
- close your eyes and imagine your guide
- write a note in your journal asking your guide to be present
- call your guide by name

Before I start doing difficult work in my journal, I will access my guide by:

....

....

....

A shield is a protective covering that keeps you safe from outside attack (or, for that matter, inside attack in the form of your Inner Critic or other parts of yourself). It can be any shape, size, color, material or weight you choose. Imagine yourself journeying along with your guide. The terrain is rocky and your footing is uncertain. Although you are being very brave, you feel scared and unsure of what might happen next. Then, BAM! Out from the shadows whizzes a flaming arrow! "SHIELD!" yells your guide. You throw up your shield, and . . . the flaming arrow fizzles, broken, to the ground.

Describe your shield below. Remember that you are making this up, so it doesn't matter if it's "right" or not. If you thought of it, it's right for you.

The shape of my shield is

....

The size of my shield is

....

The color of my shield is

....

My shield is made of

....

My shield is decorated with

....

My shield weighs

....

It is easy to carry because

....

My shield is specially crafted to protect me from

....

And it also protects me from

....

I use my shield to

....

Lighting the Way

When you're traveling down scary roads, it's important to have a source of light that you can use to illuminate the darkness and "brighten up" a fuzzy or unclear picture. Your light source also lets you know that you can **always be seen.** (If for some reason you don't want to be seen, you can always turn out your light source.)

Your light source can be—
- a flashlight
- a candle
- a lantern
- a miner's headlamp
- an oil lamp
- a torch
- an electric lamp
- the sun

Whatever it is, it's **renewable** and you don't have to worry about setting anything on fire.

My light source is

I feel safe with it because

My light source lights up

And it also lights up

I use my light source to

Even with a companion, a shield and a light source, it's important to know that you can come back to the present when it's time to quit writing. You can do this easily and comfortably when you build a bridge back to the present.

How do you build such a bridge? Well, think about the things that make you uniquely **YOU**. What are your favorite belongings or accomplishments? What tangible objects (not people or pets) do you own, use or display that help you know who you are? Think about things like:

- your college diploma
- your photo album
- your hiking boots
- your tennis racket
- your CD collection
- your car
- your very favorite sweatshirt

Now, write some of your own:

....

....

....

....

Look over your list and pick **ONE** item or symbol (please don't make it a child, spouse, friend, pet, lover, therapist or other humanoid) that can serve as your bridge to the present. Write it here:

....

I chose this symbol to be my bridge to the present because

....

....

And because

....

Now close your eyes and imagine that your "bridge" is doing just that — contorting and cartooning and stretching and twisting and growing and expanding and . . . and . . . and . . . until it becomes (in your imagination) an actual bridge from **where you were** in your journal journey to **where you are**, a real-live, grown-up, adult person on the Planet Earth.

Now, in your mind's eye, walk across this bridge. YOU MADE IT! You're back!

Additional Resources

Building A Journal Therapy Library

* *Adams, Kathleen.* **Journal to the Self: 22 Paths to Personal Growth.** Basic Three. A comprehensive yet basic book featuring a technique approach to journal writing and a focus on the therapeutic benefits of reflective writing. Very user-friendly.

Albert, Susan Wittig. **Writing From Life.** A guided writing program to tell the soul's story.

* *Baldwin, Christina.* **One to One: Self-Understanding Through Journal Writing** (Beginner Basic Three) and **Life's Companion: Journal Writing as Spiritual Quest** (Advanced Basic Three). An updated version of the former, a classic first published in 1975, came out in 1992. The latter is an exquisite synthesis of the author's life-long commitment to consciousness.

Biffle, Christopher. **A Journey Through Your Childhood.** Guided writing and art exercises for remembering childhood events. Although directed at those with "normal" childhoods, many of the exercises are excellent to help restore memory deficits for adults abused as children.

Capacchione, Lucia. **The Creative Journal** (and several others). Combination of art/non-dominant hand/dialogue exercises. Good for exploring artistic expression in the journal. See also **The Power of the Other Hand** on non-dominant hand writing.

Daniel, Lois. **How to Write Your Own Life Story.** An excellent step-by-step approach to autobiographical writing.

Davis, Laura. **The Courage to Heal Workbook.** Wise and compassionate guidance for anyone who is discovering and recovering from childhood sexual abuse.

Fox, John. **Finding What You Didn't Lose** and **Poetic Medicines.** Two excellent and very reader-friendly books that make the writing and reading of poetry accessible as a tool for growth and healing.

Goldberg, Bonni. **Room to Write.** An invigorating collection of writing prompts, especially useful for creative writing.

Hagan, Kay Leigh. **Internal Affairs** and **Prayers to the Moon.** Two effective works for unlayering the "authentic self."

Holzer, Burghild Nina. **A Walk Between Heaven and Earth.** An exquisite exploration of journal writing as a meditation and creative process.

Keen, Sam and Valley-Fox, Anne. **Your Mythic Journey.** Finding meaning in your life through writing and story-telling.

Lucas, Patty. **The Land of Tears is a Secret Place: A Loss/Grief Journal Workbook.** Compassionate guidance for active grief from a leading New Thought minister.

Mallon, Thomas. **A Book of One's Own: People and Their Diaries.** A witty and wide-ranging exploration of the art and history of diary writing.

Metzger, Deena. **Writing for Your Life.** A thorough exploration of the nature of creativity and the healing which comes from writing your own stories, both personal and mythic.

Moffat, Mary Jane and Painter, Charlotte, eds. **Revelations: Diaries of Women.** A fascinating anthology of excerpts from the famous, the semi-famous and the unknown.

Nin, Anais. **The Diary of Anais Nin, Vols. I-VII.** Nin virtually single-handedly vaulted the diary to its status as legitimate literature through the publication of her intense, intricate and utterly fascinating diaries.

Oshinsky, James. **The Discovery Journal.** An excellent workbook for teens and older kids, comprehensive yet engaging, by a school psychologist.

Pennebaker, James. **Opening Up.** Contains Dr. Pennebaker's landmark research on the relation between writing and increased immune system functioning.

Progoff, Ira. **At a Journal Workshop** and **The Practice of Process Meditation.** The texts for the famous Intensive Journal Workshops, by the original journal therapist.

* *Rainer, Tristine.* **The New Diary.** Basic Three. An excellent, thorough, and eminently readable work that covers all the bases.

Rainer, Tristine. **Your Life as Story.** An excellent guide to a serious treatment of life story and autobiography.

Schneider, Pat. **The Writer as an Artist.** An excellent collection of writing exercises that focus on developing authentic voice and equality.

Shiwy, Marlene. **A Voice of Her Own.** The journeys and journals of literary and contemporary women bring a feminist perspective to our own.

Solly, Richard and Lloyd, Roseann. **JourneyNotes.** Especially helpful for those in 12-Step addictions recovery programs.

Stillman, Peter R. **Families Writing.** Over 60 ideas to help a family share stories, record special moments, work through crises and develop lasting family ties.

Wakefield, Dan. **The Story of Your Life: Writing a Spiritual Autobiography.** A step-by-step approach to exploring your past and understanding your present through spiritual autobiography.

* The "Basic Three": The foundation for any journal library.

Books not available through the Sidran Foundation Bookshelf (see page 83), or your local bookseller, may be ordered by calling 800-833-9327.

Ten Reasons Why Journal Writing is a Powerful Adjunct to Therapy

1. **Immediacy** and **availability**. The opening paragraph of **Journal to the Self** addresses these concepts: "For nearly 30 years I have had the same therapist. This therapist is available to me 24 hours a day and hasn't gone on vacation in almost three decades. I have called upon my therapist at three in the morning, on my wedding day, on my lunch break, on a cold and lonely Christmas, on a Bora Bora beach, and in the dentist's reception room."

2. **Catharsis.** Catharsis — a safe and structured place to scream without judgment, comment or reprisal — is invaluable during the recovery/healing process. "Rather than taking a gun and shooting it wildly into the street," writes one journalkeeper, "I 'shoot the gun' in the journal, close the book tightly, and go on."[1]

3. **Object constancy.** People in recovery from trauma often have difficulty establishing and maintaining relationships. They have diminished capacity to trust that they can have a source of lasting positive presence. An ongoing relationship with a journal — a consistent presence that does not abandon, judge or punish — builds confidence and consistency.

4. **Repetition.** A vital part of the healing process is breaking silence, or telling the story of the abuse. As Davis and Bass[2] say, "Tell your story until you're finished telling it. Then tell it a few more times." The journal never tires of a story repeated dozens of times; it doesn't flinch at the 42nd beginning to an Unsent Letter. The journal, in fact, *fills up and becomes more* in the process of the repetition.

5. **Reality check.** Does writing it down make it real? Yes and no. As Davis[3] says, "There was something about putting the words on paper that made me really believe they were true." Especially during the denial stages of healing, it is important to have a tangible way of talking about what happened. While it isn't literally true that "writing it down makes it real," a written record makes denial difficult to maintain. As Bob Dylan put it, "I'm just whispering to myself so I can't pretend that I don't know."[4]

6. **Self-pacing.** Some journalkeepers fill up one notebook in a year. Others write one notebook a week. Some log only objective data. Others purge and cathart and rip holes in the paper working through their anger, confusion and grief. *There is no right or wrong way to journal.* The permission to let the journal be however it is at that moment, knowing full well that it may change in five minutes, or next week, or after springtime comes again, can be a powerful way of building self-acceptance and tolerance for change.

7. **Self-esteem.** Once initial discomfort and resistance to writing are overcome, nearly every journalkeeper finds that writing can be a reassuring, nurturing outlet for thoughts and feelings. Creative

[1]Rainer, T. *The New Diary.*
[2]Davis, L. and Bass, E., *The Courage to Heal.*
[3]Davis, L. *The Courage to Heal Workbook.*
[4] Dylan, B. *Mama You've Been On My Mind.*

expression is inherently healing, builds confidence and enhances self-esteem.

8. **Clarity and commitment.** The process of reflective writing has a cumulative effect. Patterns unfold like the seasons of the year, and recognition of cycles leads to clarity. The journal serves as a testament to new commitment: *I no longer have to be a victim. I will no longer stuff my anger. I will express myself assertively and appropriately when I begin to feel abused.*

9. **A witness to healing.** The journal provides an ongoing record of the therapeutic and recovery process. Months and years later, old volumes of the journal offer documentation and assurance that time passes, wounds heal, and circumstances change.

10. **Insight orientation.** Journal writing is a powerful media for discovering the answers that lie within each of us. As the relationship with the journal evolves, the wisdom and grace of the True Self emerge.

> In moments of ecstasy, in moments of despair
> the journal remains an impassive, silent friend,
> forever ready to coach, to confront, to critique,
> to console. Its potential as a tool
> for holistic mental health
> is unsurpassed.

Unless otherwise indicated, recommended books are resources for both clients and therapists.

INTRODUCTION

Reflective writing can be used effectively with clients at most developmental skill levels and with a broad variety of therapeutic issues and tasks. As with any effective therapy, it's important to match the journal intervention to the client's ability to master it. Low-functioning clients will be served by structured, concrete journal tasks (workbooks, Clustering, Sentence Stems, short lists, Letters, Logs, etc.). High-functioning clients can effectively use more insight-oriented techniques (Dialogue, Perspectives, Lists of 100, etc.). Permission to write without rules and acceptance of what is written without judgment or criticism are key factors in an effective journal relationship. It is also very strongly recommended that any therapist who uses the journal extensively with clients write her or his own journal. Basic instruction on journal techniques is available in my first book, JOURNAL TO THE SELF. The JOURNAL TO THE SELF workshop is taught throughout the United States and Canada by instructors certified through The Center for Journal Therapy. Call or write for the names of Certified Instructors in your area or for information on the home-study Instructor Certification Program. The JOURNAL TO THE SELF workshop is also available on cassette tape.

ADDICTIONS

The journal can serve as a bridge into a new lifestyle, a place to ventilate the edginess and restlessness that are part of early-stage withdrawal and recovery, and a record for the future of how sobriety has been achieved and maintained "one page at a time." Since feeling states are often numbed or avoided through substance abuse, becoming acquainted with emotions is another task well-suited for journal work. If the client is working a 12-Step program (Alcoholics Anonymous, Adult Children of Alcoholics, Cocaine Anonymous, Overeaters Anonymous, Incest Survivors Anonymous, etc.) the journal is a safe and private place for the self-examination inherent in the individual steps. Recommended reading: **Journey Notes: Writing for Recovery and Spiritual Growth**, Richard Solly and Roseann Lloyd; there are also several good 12-Step workbooks available.

ADOLESCENTS

Creativity and fantasy are both excellent entrees. Suggest Alpha-Poems; other poetic forms; art; collage. Artistic productions can be titled and accompanied by a written interpretation. Fantasy and symbolic or metaphoric writing are appealing to teens. Guided imagery works well in groups. Workbooks provide helpful structure, and **The Discovery Journal** by Dr. James Oshinksy is excellent. Confidentiality and privacy are crucial issues for the adolescent. Help teens with problem-solving on how to set boundaries around the journal, and if necessary and appropriate, intervene at the fam-

ily level to advocate for privacy agreements. Parents are much less likely to invade a teenager's journal if they are keeping journals themselves. Suggest a "community journal" or "dialogue journal" for the entire family. Recommended reading: **The Castle of the Pearl** and **A Journey Through Your Childhood,** both by Christopher Biffle; **The Discovery Journal,** James Oshinsky. See also **Families.**

AGING

Autobiographical or "life story" writing can be a delightful and gratifying activity for older people. Writing can be painful for arthritic hands/shoulders and aging eyes; keep handwritten tasks brief. Give focused and structured suggestions: Write a story about a memorable childhood Christmas, how your parents met, what first grade was like, how you met your spouse, the war years, the Depression, the birth of your first child. Alternatives to writing: Talking into a tape recorder, telling the story while a family member or volunteer transcribes. If you are leading a group of elders in an exercise, keep verbal instructions brief and clear. Recommended reading: **How to Write Your Own Life Story,** Lois Daniels.

AIDS

The therapeutic tasks for people with HIV/AIDS and their families/partners/caregivers include dealing with strong emotions; meaning-of-life issues; holistic living with AIDS; dealing with grief; forgiveness; with the advent of new medications, learning to treat HIV as a long-term chronic illness; and, eventually, life closure. Lists of 100 (Things I've Accomplished in My Lifetime, Things I Want to Do While I Can) can help with clarity and focus. Unsent (or Sent!) Letters can help with communication and closure. A life review through spiritual autobiography can be a meaningful task. A community journal co-created with caregivers/loved ones is a precious legacy. Recommended reading: **The Story of Your Life: Writing a Spiritual Autobiography,** Dan Wakefield; any of the increasing presence of autobiographical books about living and dying with AIDS. See also: **Anger; Grief/Loss; Spiritual Issues.**

ANGER

Unsent Letters (uncensored, unedited) are a good device, as is a List of 100 (Reasons I'm Mad, Things You've Done That Are Outrageous, Things I Wish I'd Said, Behaviors I Will No Longer Tolerate, etc.). Emphasize that pressured writing (both physically and emotionally) is both natural and appropriate. It is sometimes appropriate and helpful to symbolize the release of the anger by destroying the journal entry after it has been completed (e.g., wadding it up and stomping on it, tearing it, burning it in an ashtray or fireplace). This also guards against possible retaliatory acting out by actually delivering or sharing a journal entry written in anger; however, it is important not to communicate the message that anger in the journal is not acceptable. Anger discharged in the journal is most effectively accompanied by movement to release energy. Suggest exercise, pillow-pounding, dancing aerobically around the living room.

Recommended reading: **Dr. Weisinger's Anger Work-Out Book**, Dr. H. Weisinger.

ANXIETY DISORDERS
The journal can help reality-test by recording and challenging cognitive distortions, irrational ideas, thought-stopping, and other behavioral/rational-emotive techniques. Keeping lists and logs provide structuring and organizing functions. Notations can also be made after self-relaxation techniques (breathing, self-hypnosis, relaxation tapes) to reinforce positive change. Recommended reading: **The Feeling Good Handbook**, David Burns; **The Relaxation and Stress Reduction Workbook**, Matthew McKay, et al.; **Thoughts and Feelings: The Art of Cognitive Stress Intervention**, Matthew McKay, et al.

BIPOLAR ILLNESS
See **Depression** and **Mania.**

CHILDREN
Young children will likely lack consistency in their journalkeeping. Offer a notebook all their own, and communicate your willingness to help. Use the journal to teach about privacy, boundaries and independent thinking. Don't push kids to write or share. When they do, listen carefully and with curiosity. Some traumatized children are fearful of committing "secrets" to paper, while others use writing as a clever sidestep to "not telling." Offer to write down their words as they tell the story, or extend an invitation to draw the story. Older children do well with Sentence Stems or other fill-in-the-blank structures. Recommended reading: **The Creative Journal for Children**, Lucia Capacchione; **The Discovery Journal**, James Oshinsky. See **Families.**

CHRONIC OR LIFE-THREATENING ILLNESS
See **AIDS, Grief/Loss.**

CO-DEPENDENCY
Building self-esteem and exploring options are primary tasks for breaking free from unhealthy relationships. The journal can become a living metaphor for the emerging relationship with Self. Journal groups work exceptionally well for people who are seeking healthier ways to meet relatedness and connection needs. Recommended reading: **Internal Affairs: A Journalkeeping Workbook for Self-Intimacy** and **Prayers to the Moon: Exercises in Self-Reflection**, both by Kay Leigh Hagan.

DEPRESSION
Journal writing can provide a sense of task-orientation and accomplishment when immobilization sets in. Although process work in the journal is often helpful to identify the patterns and themes of the depression, one who is chronically depressed is susceptible to reinforcement of futility when only the somberness is recorded. Limiting reflective writing to only the "bad stuff" also has the effect of

negatively conditioning the writer to the journal. Advocate for balance in the journal through "win lists" or "victory logs" of anything that is going right; Captured Moments of happier times or even the smallest accomplishments; medication logs to note shifts with pharmacological intervention. Recommended reading: **The Feeling Good Handbook**, David Burns; **Journaling for Joy**, Joyce Chapman.

DISSOCIATIVE DISORDERS

Recovering "lost" time and recalling "lost" experiences are keys to permeating the dissociative barriers. A journal can document activities, thoughts, and feelings during blacked-out or dissociated episodes. Suggest that the client time-date each entry at both the start and the end of the entry and write three feeling words at either end. Writing with the non-dominant hand is *not* recommended, as this technique is very effective in revealing suppressed or disowned material and can be difficult to contain and pace. Because of the acuity and complexity of the material recovered in the journal, it is useful to help patients structure their journal tasks by suggesting appropriate boundaries. This can be as simple as using the notebook page as a boundary ("be sure to leave yourself margins") or developing writing exercises that are time- and length-limited. Recommended reading: **A Journey Through Your Childhood**, Christopher Biffle; **The Power of Your Other Hand**, Lucia Capacchione; **Journal to the Self**, Kathleen Adams; **MPD From the Inside Out**, Barry Cohen, Esther Giller, Lynn W., eds. See also **Incest/Sexual Abuse, Ritual/Sadistic Abuse.**

DREAM INTERPRETATION

Journal dreamwork begins, of course, with logging the dream upon awakening. Most journal techniques used for the "waking life" can be adapted for dream interpretation. Try Clusters or Dialogues with dream symbols or characters, Stream of Consciousness about the dream itself, Perspectives entries written from the symbol/character's point of view, Clustering with dream material. Recommended reading: **Journal to the Self**, Kathleen Adams; anything by Jeremy Taylor.

DYSFUNCTIONAL FAMILY OF ORIGIN

The journal environment — safe, structured, consistent, accepting, non-judgmental — shows a marked contrast to the environment in which a typical Adult Child grew up. Captured Moments provide clarity on childhood experiences, especially when combined with the Perspectives technique of writing from the child's point of view. Character Sketches of parents and intimate partners can help identify patterns of relatedness. Dialogues with Inner Child or Inner Teacher can be useful. The journal can be the perfect vehicle to help the hurt and lonely child inside grow up into a healthy, happy adult. Suggested reading: **A Workbook for Healing: Adult Children of Alcoholics**, Patty McConnell.

EATING DISORDERS

The journal can give voice to the messages conveyed by the eating behavior. The symbolism of food can be explored through Dialogue. Behavior/affect charts can document cognitive approaches. The journal provides a stage for "dress rehearsals" of situations, conversations, confrontations, behaviors. A combination journal/photo album helps to re-establish a relationship with body image. Collages are also very effective in addressing body image. Suggested reading: **Feeding the Hungry Heart** and anything else by Geneen Roth.

FAMILIES

A family writing program can open communication in a meaningful and gentle way. "Dialogue journals" or "community journals" are, in the words of one keeper, ". . . a good place to play with scraps of life." Such journals, as the name suggest, invite each family member to write randomly or responsively about issues ranging from mundane "scraps of life" to profound problem-solving and negotiation. An excellent way to reinforce teachings about active listening, "I" messages and conflict resolution. There are also many fun and rewarding family writing exercises that can weave into a priceless legacy for future generations. Suggested reading: **Families Writing**, Peter B. Stillman.

GRIEF/LOSS

For the newly bereaved, feelings are so close to the surface and pain is so raw that short, structured journal exercises offer the most comfort. Clustering ("Who am I now?" is a good exercise that addresses changing roles and lifestyles) and Unsent Letters to the deceased are both manageable tasks. There is something comforting and reassuring about documenting the movement through time in the early stages. Brief daily Time Capsule entries are often helpful. Captured Moments can also be used to explore the mental snapshots the bereaved remembers about the loved one or the process of dying. With anticipatory grief, lists of "What I Love About You" or "What I Want to Thank You For" or letters can facilitate closure. Recommended reading: **The Land of Tears is a Secret Place: A Grief/Loss Support Journal Workbook**, Rev. Patty Lucas.

GUILT/SHAME See **Dysfunctional Family of Origin, Incest/Sexual Abuse.**

INCEST/SEXUAL ABUSE

Some of the therapeutic tasks for recovery from incest and sexual abuse are to explore feelings, mourn violation, gather strength and celebrate healing. Each of these tasks (which often overlap) adapts well to journal work. Writing about memories of abuse allows the client to define her or his own reality, perhaps for the first time, without minimization or distortion. Non-dominant hand writing will frequently access repressed feelings (terror, rage, debilitating shame); teach clients how to pace so that they don't become overwhelmed. Reading the writings of other incest survivors can be a powerful and affirming way of breaking silence and is often the ap-

propriate starting place. Recommended reading: **The Courage to Heal**, Ellen Bass and Laura Davis; **The Courage To Heal Workbook**, Davis; **I Never Told Anyone**, Bass. See also **Dissociative Disorders, Sadistic Abuse.**

MANIA

Many clues to manic states can be picked up just by carefully observing the journal. Clues include: unusually high volume; physically pressured writing that gives texture to both the front and back side of the page; rapid and erratic shifts in penmanship; consistent use of sentence fragments or incomplete thoughts; crowded writing that ignores margins; sprawled or large writing. Often, the journal is perceived as a "best friend" or "necessary for my sanity." This is a mixed blessing. The journal can serve as a container for uncontrollable energy and a release for internal pressure, but in the process it may bring up a steady stream of overstimulation without appropriate pacing. Suggest tasks that help with pacing and organization, as well as relaxation techniques that can be logged and documented. Some rational-emotive strategies work well. Teach relaxation in conjunction with journal sessions. See **Anxiety Disorders.**

PSYCHOSIS
See **Thought Disorders.**

SADISTIC ABUSE

In the early stages of uncovering awareness of sadistic abuse, the primary task is to create safety and structure in the journal. Most sadistic abuse survivors will be decidedly averse — sometimes to the point of immobilization — to the concept of committing to writing the atrocities they experienced. Because these sadistic abuses were often accompanied with threats of terrible consequences if the secrets were told, the idea of leaving a paper trail is perceived as potentially life-threatening. Warm-ups to the journal can include writing about non-sensitive material, daily events, objective logs of happenings, a "win list" or "victory log" of things that are going well, and other "non-classified" information. Once this is accomplished, the journal can serve as a way to contain the memories and abreact the trauma by "writing through." It is vitally necessary to "build the container" by helping the patient learn entry, exit and pacing skills. Use imagery and metaphor to help patients find a benevolent guide, a protective shield, a light source for illumination, and a bridge back to the present. See also **Dissociative Disorders, Incest/Sexual Abuse.**

SCHIZOPHRENIA
See **Thought Disorders.**
SPIRITUAL ISSUES

Clients who are exploring spiritual issues are good candidates for any of the insight-oriented techniques. Dialogues with Higher Self (Inner Wisdom, Higher Power, the Teacher Within, etc.) can provide clarity and guidance. Meditation logs or prayer journals can be comforting, insightful and revealing. Guided imagery and dream work are powerful. Stepping Stones provide opportunities for interpretation of life path, as does writing personal mythology. Recommended reading: **Your Mythic Journey,** Sam Keen and Anne Valley-Fox; **The Story of Your Life,** Dan Wakefield; **Life's Companion: Journal Writing as Spiritual Quest,** Christina Baldwin. See also: **Dream Interpretation.**

THOUGHT DISORDERS

Journal writing is **not** always the tool of choice for thought disorders, as it requires cognitive structuring that is often not available. The result is frequently written "word salad" or bizarre production, which can be more disorganizing and decompensating. If writing is used at all, try highly structured and short techniques such as Clustering or Sentence Stems. Patients who attempt writing in a psychotic state report that it can contribute to feeling frightened, decompensated, vulnerable and unprotected. Still, there is sometimes a drive to express; poetry or art helps contain and communicate the inner world.

About The Author

Kathleen (Kay) Adams, M.A., L.P.C. is a licensed psychotherapist, author, educator and internationally acclaimed pioneer in journal therapy. She designs and implements journal therapy programs in hospitals, recovery centers, and mental health clinics throughout the United States and Canada. Kay is a frequent presenter at professional conferences and represents journal therapists on the Board of Directors of the National Association of Poetry Therapy. She is on the faculty of several institutes, including the Omega Institute and the New York Open Center.

The Center for Journal Therapy, founded by Kay Adams in 1985, is dedicated to teaching the healing art of journal writing to individuals, groups and mental health professionals. The Center publishes a newsletter, *The Wave,* and offers trainings in clinical journal therapy for helping professionals.

Please write, call, or fax for information on:
• journal therapy consultations
• program design and implementation for hospitals and treatment centers
• faculty appointments for institutes, seminars and conferences
• workshops and trainings
• Journal to the Self Instructor Certification Training

Kathleen Adams, M.A., L.P.C.
The Center for Journal Therapy
PO Box 963
Arvada, CO 80001
toll-free phone 888-421-2298
fax 303-421-1255

To learn more about language arts therapies, or for information about credentialing in developmental or clinical journal/poetry therapy write:
The National Association for Poetry Therapy
Dept. CJT
PO Box 551
Port Washington, NY 11050

Also by Kathleen Adams
JOURNAL TO THE SELF: 22 Paths to Personal Growth (Warner Books)

SIDRAN INSTITUTE

About the SIDRAN INSTITUTE

The Sidran Institute, a leader in traumatic stress education and advocacy, is a nationally focused nonprofit organization devoted to helping people understand, manage, and treat traumatic stress. Our education and advocacy promotes greater understanding of:

- The early recognition and treatment of trauma-related stress in children;
- The understanding of trauma and its long-term effect on adults;
- The strategies leading to greatest success in self-help recovery for trauma survivors;
- The clinical methods and practices leading to greatest success in aiding trauma victims;
- The development of public policy initiatives that are responsive to the needs of adult and child survivors of traumatic events.

To further this mission, Sidran operates the following programs:

The Sidran Institute Press publishes books and educational materials on traumatic stress and dissociative conditions. A recently published example is *Growing Beyond Survival: A Self-Help Toolkit for Managing Traumatic Stress,* by Elizabeth Vermilyea. This innovative workbook provides skill-building tools to empower survivors to take control of their trauma symptoms.

Some of our other titles include *Risking Connection: A Training Curriculum for Working with Survivors of Childhood Abuse* (a curriculum for mental health professionals and paraprofessionals), *Managing Traumatic Stress Through Art* (an interactive workbook to promote healing), and *The Twenty-Four Carat Buddha and Other Fables: Stories of Self-Discovery.*

The Sidran Bookshelf on Trauma and Dissociation is an annotated mail order and web catalog of the best in clinical, educational, and survivor-supportive literature on post-traumatic stress, dissociative conditions, and related topics.

The Sidran Resource Center – drawing from Sidran's extensive database and library – provides information and resources at no cost to callers from around the English-speaking world. The information includes: trauma-experienced therapists, traumatic stress organizations, educational books and materials, conferences, trainings, and treatment facilities.

Sidran Training and Consultation Services provide conference speakers, pre-programmed and custom workshops, consultation, and technical assistance on all aspects of traumatic stress including:

- **Public Education and Consultation** to organizations, associations, and government on a variety of trauma topics and public education strategies.
- **Agency Training** on trauma-related topics, such as Trauma Symptom Management, Assessment and Treatment Planning, Borderline Personality Disorder, and others. We will be glad to customize presentations for the specific needs of your agency.
- **Survivor Education** programming including how to start and maintain effective peer support groups, community networking for trauma support, successful selection of therapists, coping skills, and healing skills.

For more information on any of these programs and projects, please contact us:

Sidran Institute
200 East Joppa Road, Suite 207, Baltimore, MD 21286
Phone: 410-825-8888 ▪ Fax: 410-337-0747
E-mail: sidran@sidran.org ▪ Website: **www.sidran.org**

EDUCATION ● PUBLICATIONS ● RESOURCES

LaVergne, TN USA
06 July 2010

188459LV00001B/6/P